Alfie's

Numbers

Shirley Hughes

THE BODLEY HEAD

LONDON

1

One, two, three – go!

Here's **one** little boy called Alfie,
running up the street.

Two's company.
Alfie can count and he's teaching
his little sister Annie Rose.

$$\cdot\cdot\, 2$$

2¨

It takes **two** to see-saw.

2

But when Alfie gets on, Annie Rose goes
up in the air and Alfie hits the ground
– plonk!   (I wonder why?)

2

Here are **two** pairs of shoes.
One pair is Alfie's and the other belongs
to Annie Rose. That makes one, two, three,
four shoes altogether!

2

And here are Alfie's Noah's Ark animals,
walking **two** by **two**.

3...

Three's company when friends come to play...

···3

…though sometimes Annie Rose feels left out.

3...

Alfie and his dad and the pig make **three**.

Funny old pig!

There are **four** people in Alfie's family
(not counting Chessie the cat).

But when they go on a visit to Grandma's house there are **five**.

5 .....

Five people getting ready for a party...

…and **five** balloons!

6

Six cows, browsing in a field...

6 • • • • •

...and **six** children sitting around the table at Alfie's birthday party.

Sam is *under* the table,
so that makes seven!

Seven friendly neighbours,
having tea together.

8 . . . .

Eight party children, popping bubbles.
Bubbles are light, they float in the air…

...some big, some small... too many to count when you are busy popping!

8 · · · · · · · ·

Eight people walking to work up Alfie's street. Are the same number coming home again?

If you add one little dog that makes nine.

9 · · · · · · · · ·

Nine messy bears, walking around
Alfie's bowl.

And **nine** old friends, waiting to play.

10 ··········

Ten fingers each – five on one hand
and five on the other!

And how many toes?

10 · · · · · · · · ·

Ten children playing on a big fallen tree.

And so many leaves on the trees,
and so many flowers and berries growing,

and shells and stones on the beach...

...and creatures on the earth...

...and so many stars in the sky
that we can't count them!